THE NEW BE
90's COUNTRY
FOR GUITAR

Arranged by Louis Martinez

Editor: Aaron Stang
Music Editor: Colgan Bryan
Book Design: Joseph Klucar
Photography: Roberto Santos

A GOOD RUN OF BAD LUCK

By
CLINT BLACK and HAYDEN NICHOLAS

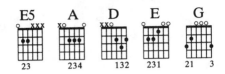

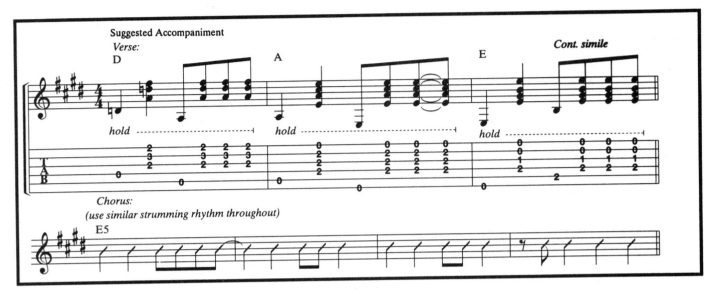

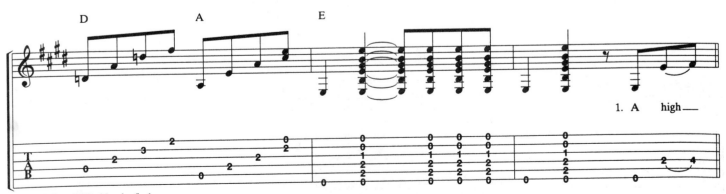

A Good Run Of Bad Luck - 5 - 1

Verses 1 & 2:

roll - er   e - ven when the chips are down.____

2. See additional lyrics

To win her o - ver   I'd seen the ta - bles turn a - round.____

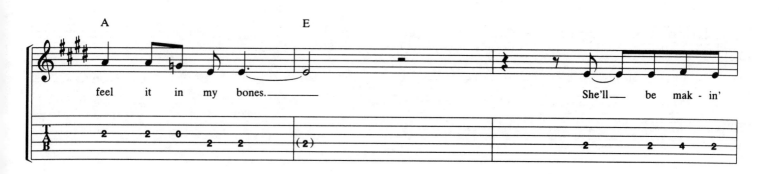

She's___ ten the hard___ way,   I can

feel it in my bones.____   She'll___ be mak - in'

my day   and not an - oth - er night a - lone.____

A Good Run Of Bad Luck - 5 - 2

4

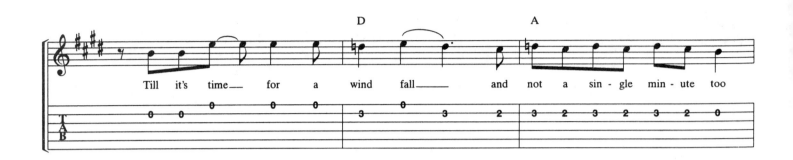

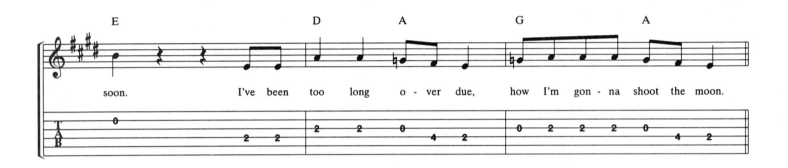

Chorus:

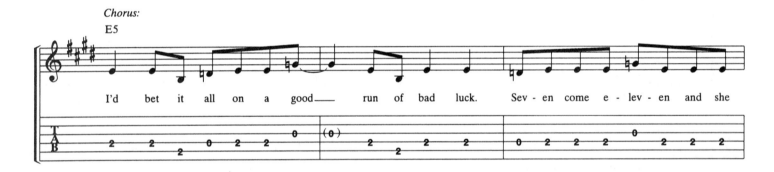

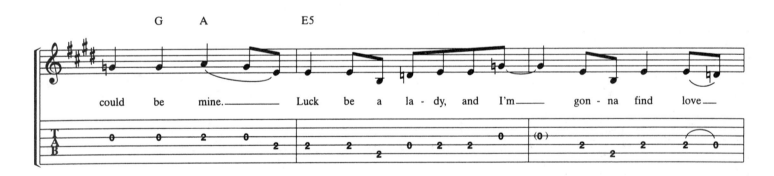

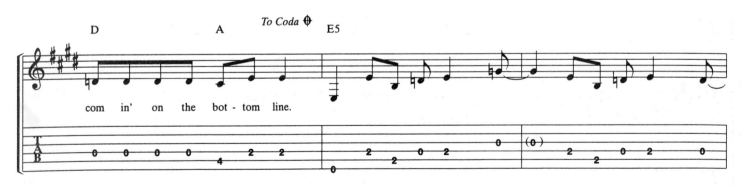

6

Verse 2:
I've been to the table, and I've lost it all before.
I'm willin' and able, always comin' back for more.
Squeezin' out a thin dime till there's no one hanging on my arm.
I've gambled on a third time, a fool will tell you it's charm.
If I'm bettin' on a loser, I'm gonna have devil to pay.
But it's the only game I know to play, it doesn't matter anyway.
(To Chorus)

A THOUSAND MILES FROM NOWHERE

Words and Music by
DWIGHT YOAKAM

9

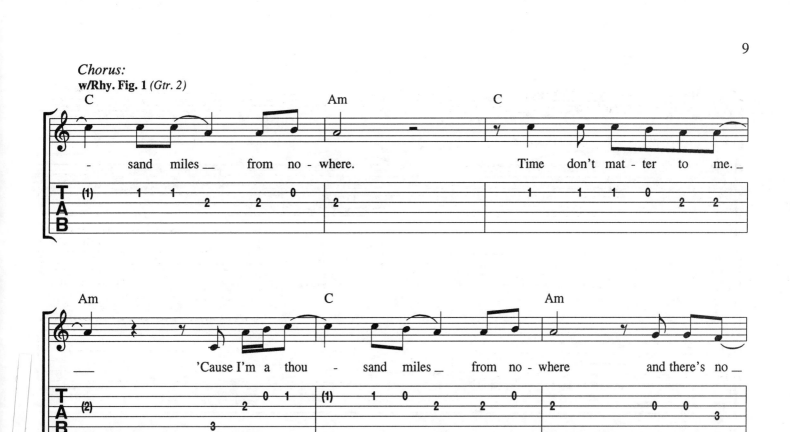

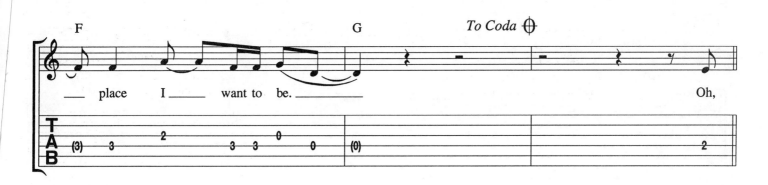

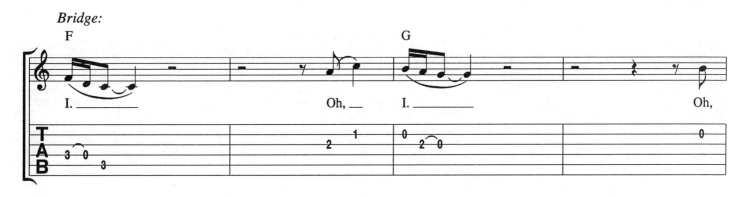

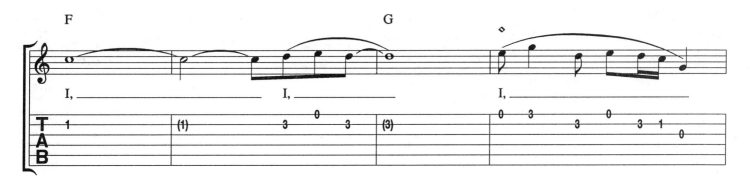

A Thousand Miles from Nowhere – 5 – 3

10

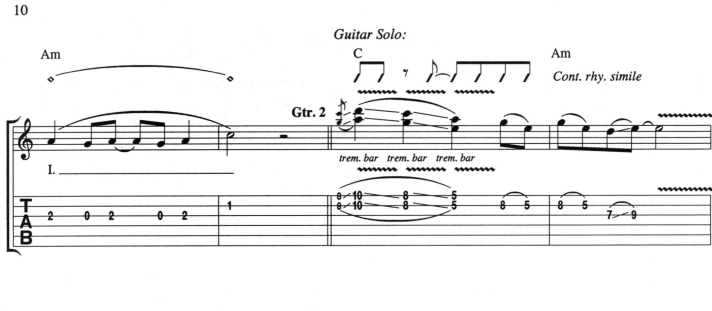

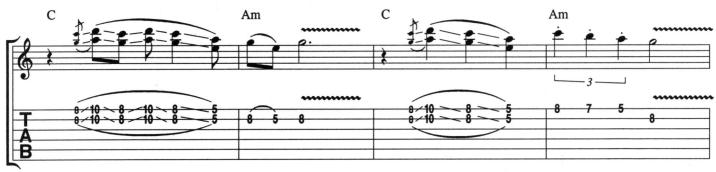

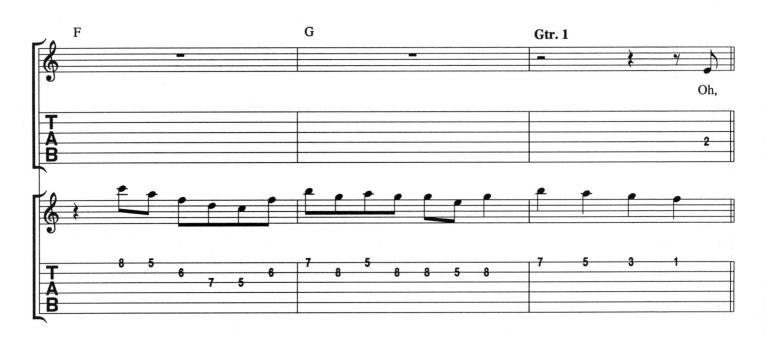

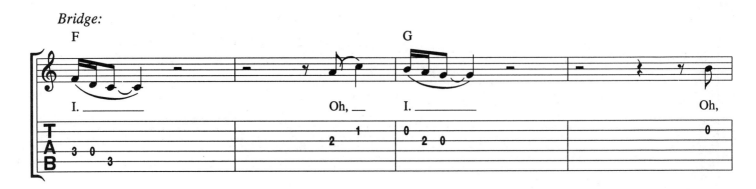

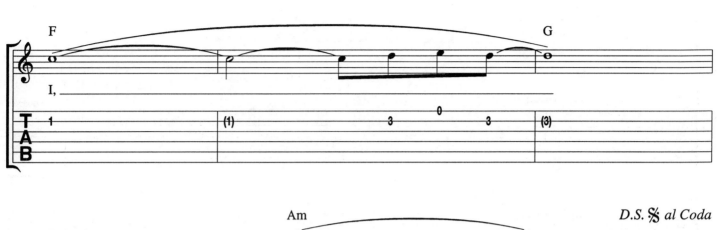

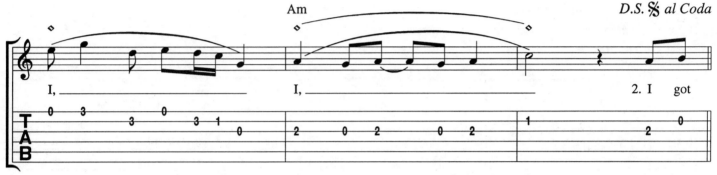

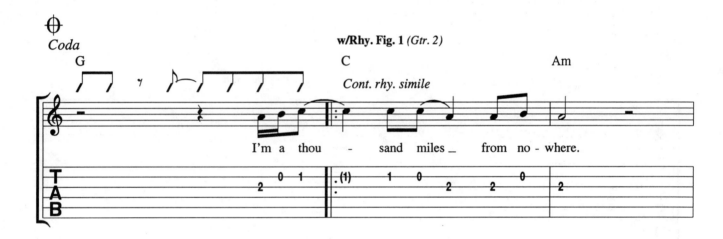

CHATTAHOOCHEE

Words and Music by
ALAN JACKSON and JIM McBRIDE

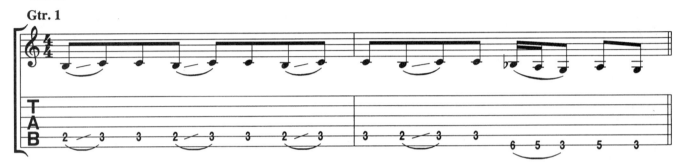

Moderately fast ♩ = 176

Intro:

Cont. rhy. simile

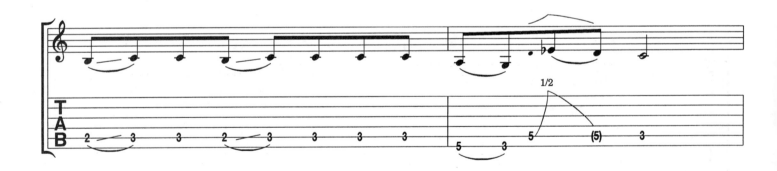

14

We laid rub - ber on the Geor - gia as - phalt, we
set - tled for a bur - ger and a grape sno - cone. I

got a lit - tle cra - zy but we nev - er got caught.
dropped her off ear - ly, but I did - n't go home.

Pre-Chorus:

Cont. rhy. simile

Down by the riv - er on a Fri - day night, _ (a) pyr - a - mid of cans in the

pale __ moon - light. Talk - ing 'bout cars and dream - in' 'bout wom - en,

nev - er had a plan, just a liv - in' for the min - ute. Yeah,

Chorus:

w/Rhy. Fig. 1 *(Gtr. 1) 2 times*

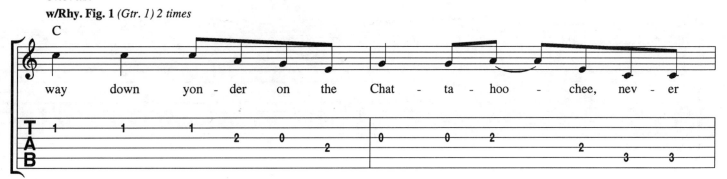

way down yon - der on the Chat - ta - hoo - chee, nev - er

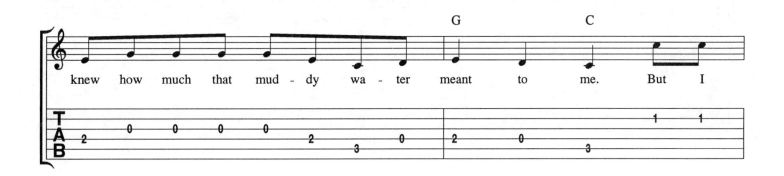

knew how much that mud - dy wa - ter meant to me. But I

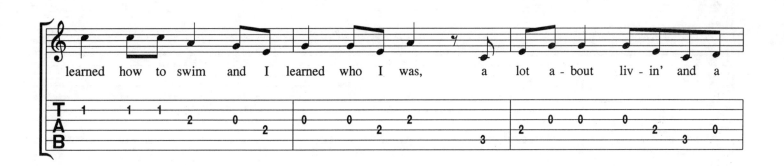

learned how to swim and I learned who I was, a lot a - bout liv - in' and a

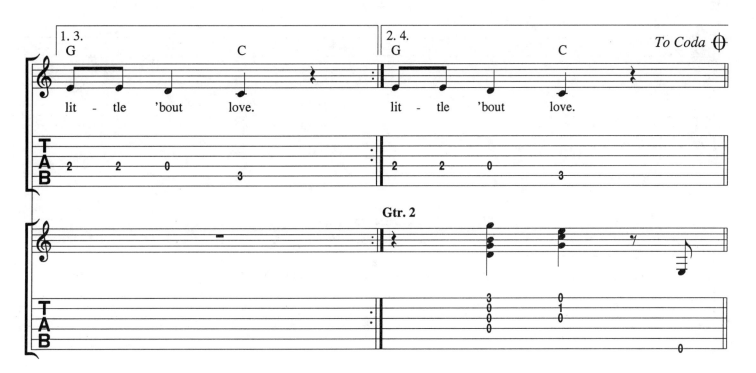

1. 3. lit - tle 'bout love.

2. 4. lit - tle 'bout love. *To Coda* ⊕

Gtr. 2

16

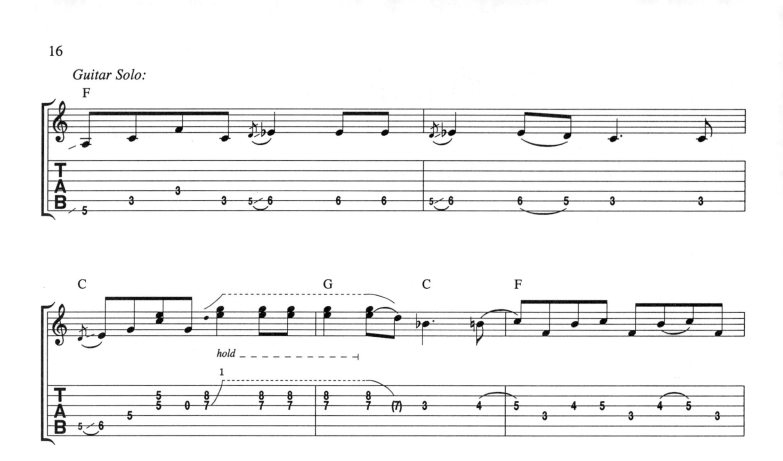

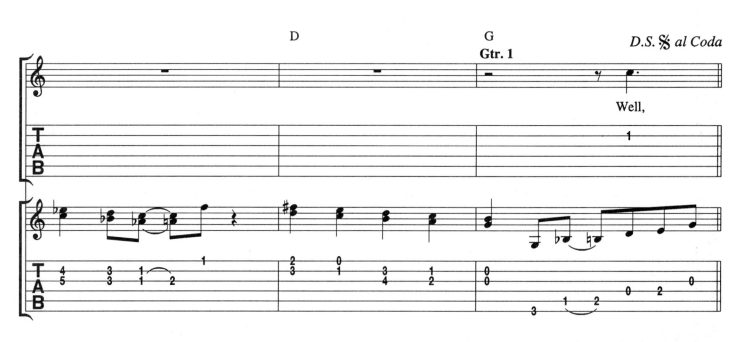

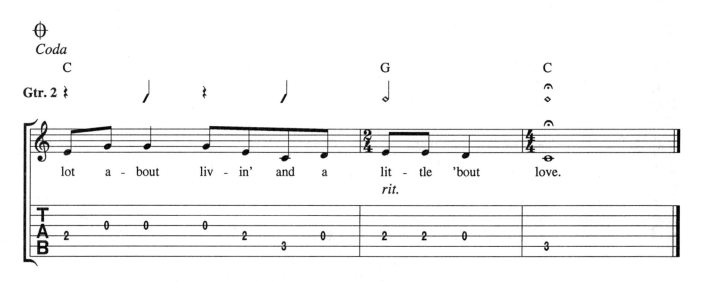

Chattahoochee – 5 – 5

FAST AS YOU

Words and Music by
DWIGHT YOAKAM

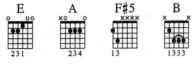

Fast as You – 5 – 1

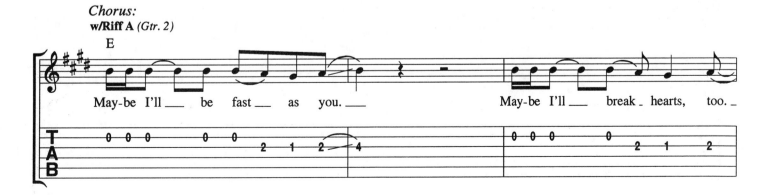

Coda

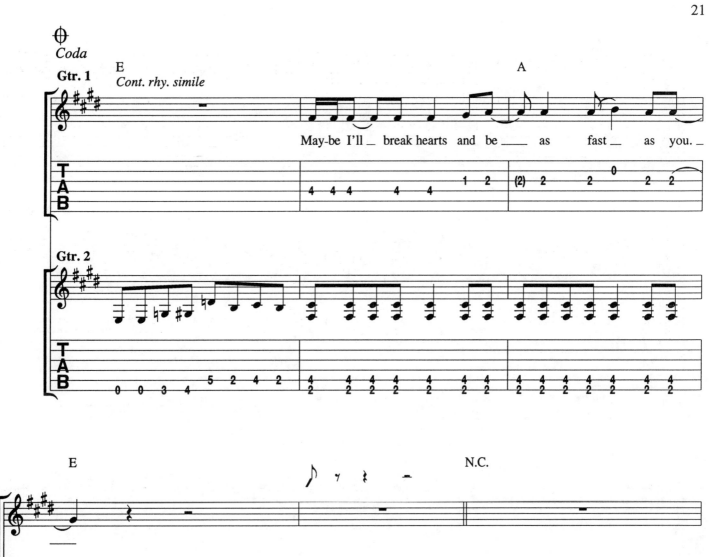

May-be I'll __ break hearts and be ____ as fast __ as you. __

I CAN'T TELL YOU WHY

Words and Music by
DON HENLEY, GLENN FREY & TIMOTHY B. SCHMIT

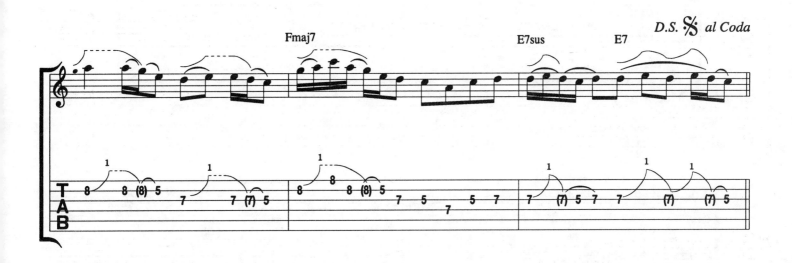

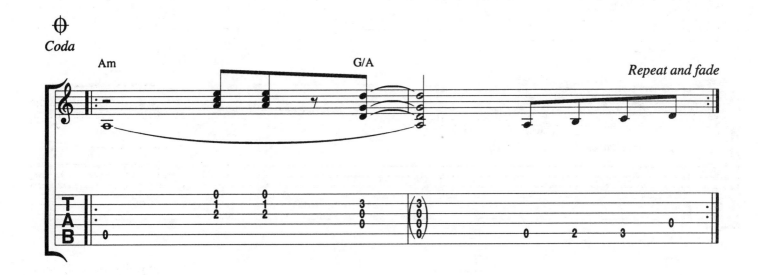

Verse 2:

When we get crazy,
It just ain't right.
Girl, I get lonely, too.
You don't have to worry.
Just hold on tight,
'Cause I love you.
Nothin's wrong as far as I can see.
We make it harder than it has to be,
And I can't tell you why.

IN LONESOME DOVE

Words and Music by
CYNTHIA LIMBAUGH and GARTH BROOKS

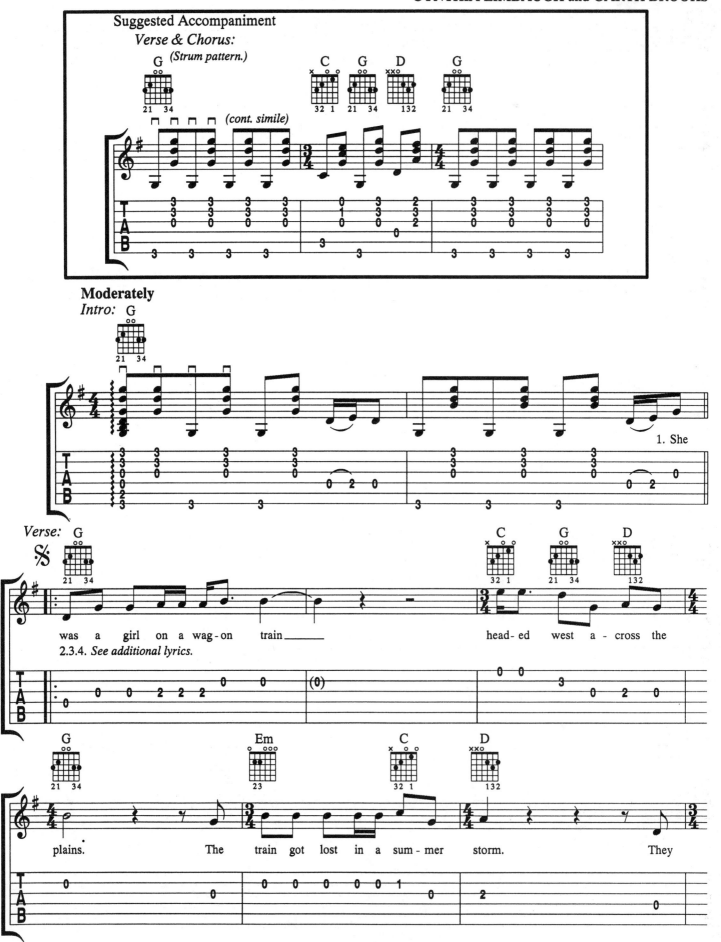

In Lonesome Dove – 4 – 1

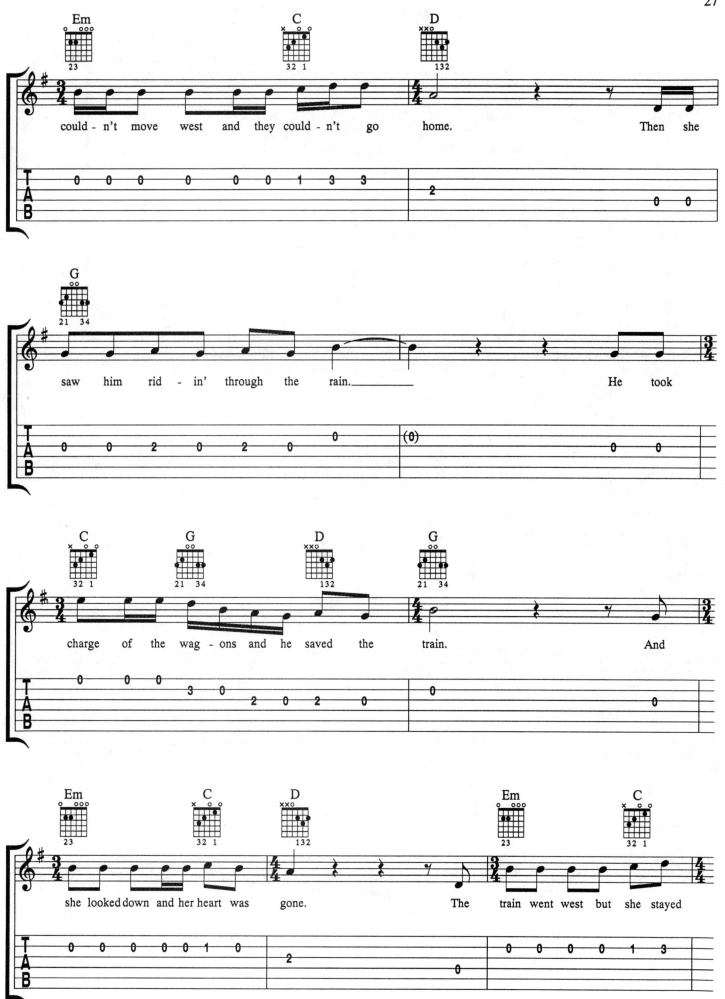

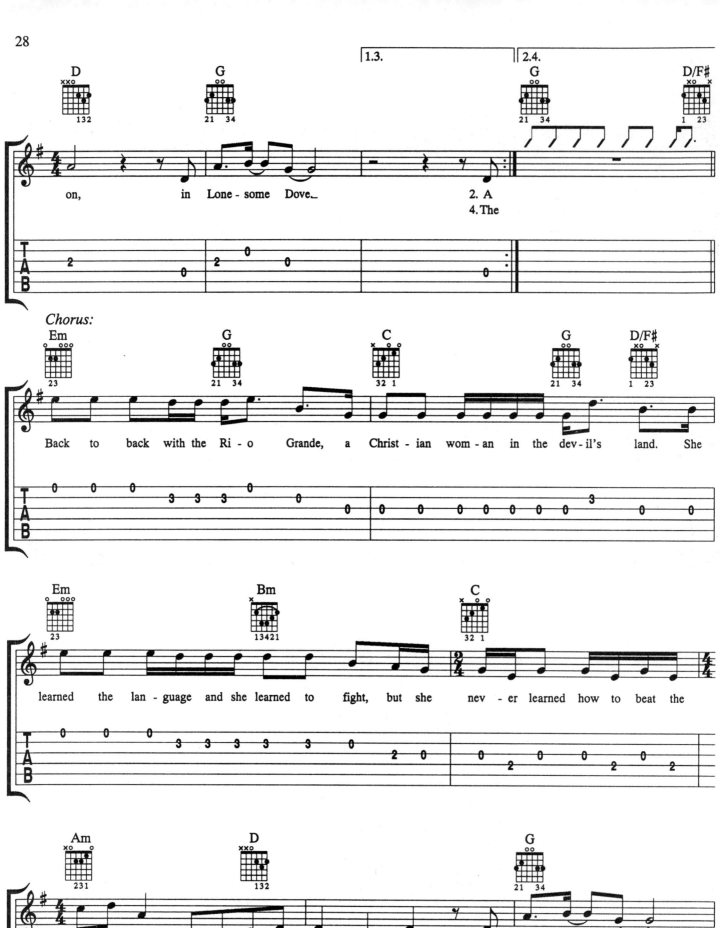

Lone - some _ Dove. _   3. She

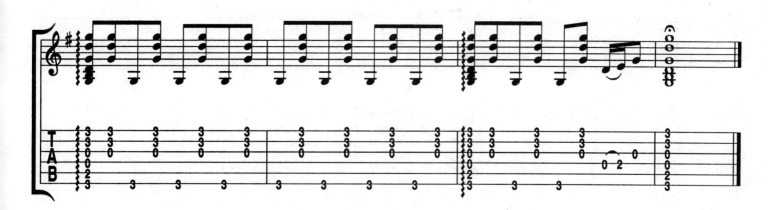

Verse 2:
A farmer's daughter with a gentle hand,
A blooming rose in a bed of sand;
She loved the man who wore a star,
A Texas Ranger known near and far.
So they got married and they had a child,
But times were tough and the West was wild.
So it was no surprise the day she learned
That her Texas man would not return
To Lonesome Dove. *(To Chorus:)*

Verse 3:
She watched her boy grow to a man.
He had an angel's heart and the devil's hand.
He wore his star for all to see.
He was a Texas lawman legacy.
Then one day word blew into town.
It seemed the men that shot his father down
Had robbed a bank in Cherico.
The only thing 'tween them and Mexico
Was Lonesome Dove. *(To Verse 4:)*

Verse 4:
The shadows stretched across the land
As the shots rang out down the Rio Grande.
And when the smoke had finally cleared the street,
The men lay at the ranger's feet.
But legend tells to this very day
That shots were comin' from an alleyway.
'Though no one knows who held the gun,
There ain't no doubt if you ask someone
In Lonesome Dove. *(To Chorus:)*

In Lonesome Dove – 4 – 4

LIZA JANE

Words and Music by
VINCE GILL and REED NIELSEN

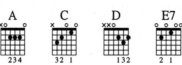

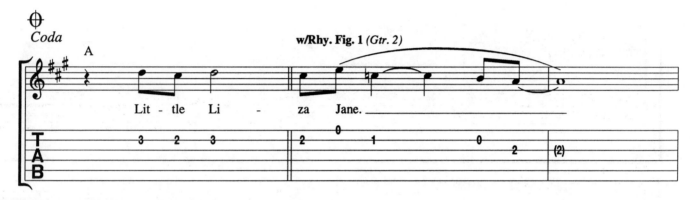

Verse 2:
You've got that body,
You've got that frame.
So, why don't you call me,
Little Liza Jane?
(To Chorus:)

Verse 3:
Now you've heard my story,
You've got to know my name.
So, why don't you call me,
Little Liza Jane?
(To Chorus:)

NO TIME TO KILL

By
CLINT BLACK and HAYDEN NICHOLAS

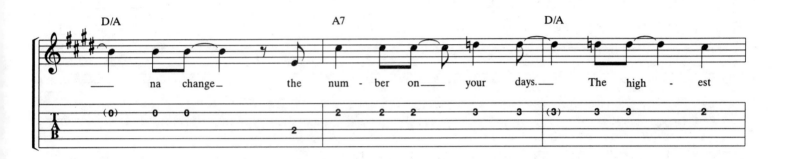

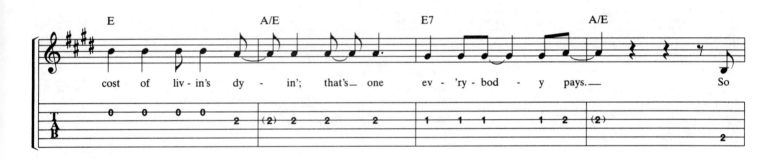

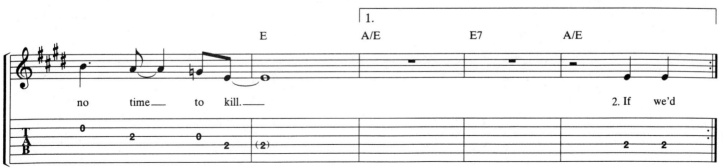

No Time To Kill - 4 - 2

36

No Time To Kill - 4 - 3

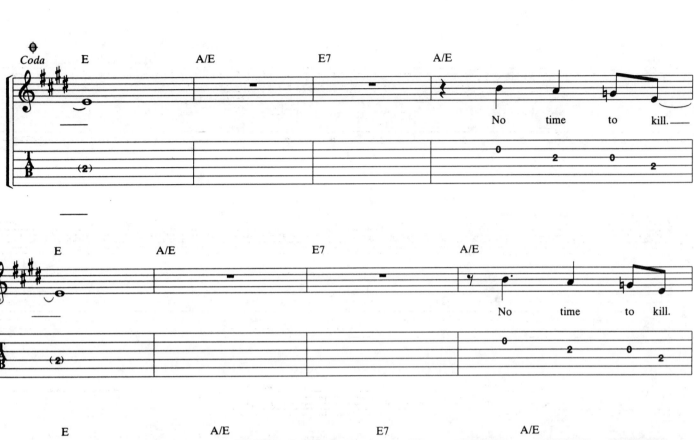

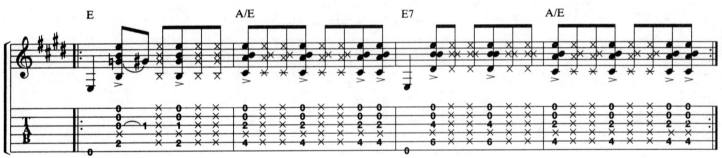

Verse 2:
If we'd known ten years ago today would be ten years from now,
Would we spend tomorrow's yesterdays and make it last somehow?
Or lead the cheers in someone else's game and never learn to play
And see the rules of thumb are all the same that measure every day.
The grass is green on both sides of the hill,
There's no time to kill.
(To Chorus:)

Verse 3:
If we had an hour glass to watch each one go by,
Or a bell to mark each one to pass,
We'd see just how they fly.
Would we escalate the value to be worth its weight in gold,
Or would we never know the fortunes that we had till we grow old?
And do we just keep killin' time until there's no time to kill?
(To Chorus:)

PUT YOURSELF IN MY SHOES

Words and Music by
CLINT BLACK, HAYDEN NICHOLAS
and SHAKE RUSSELL

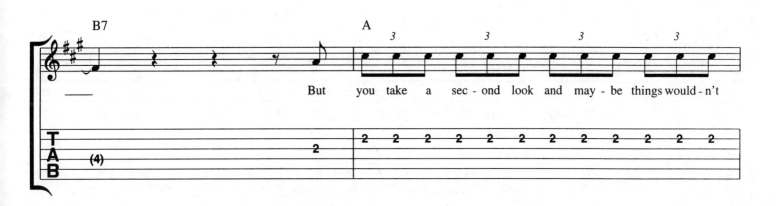

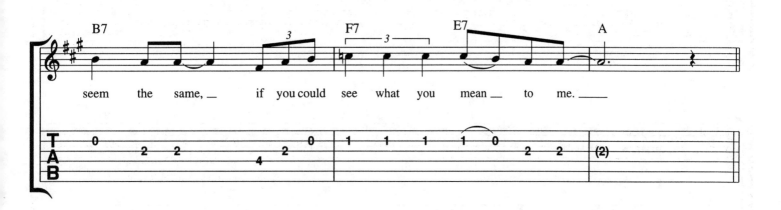

Chorus:

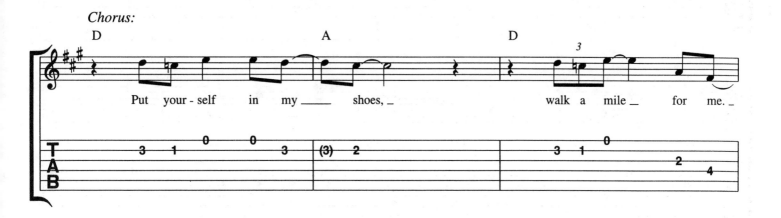

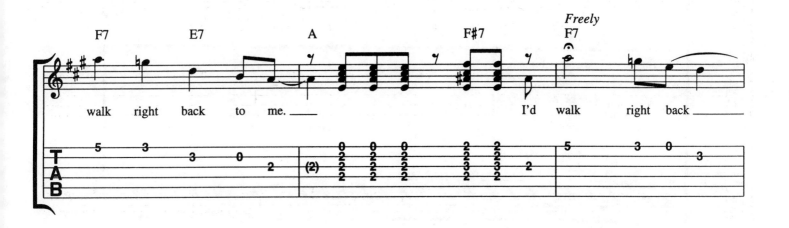

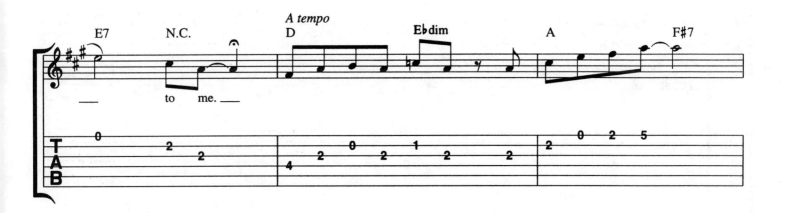

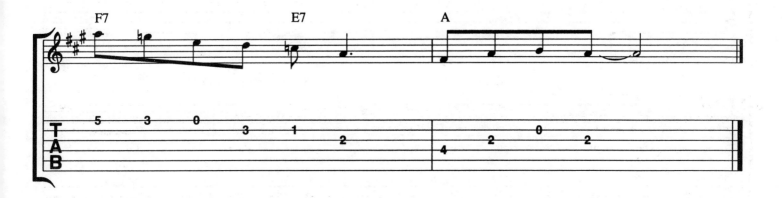

Verse 2: You're gonna keep walkin' and you're gonna pass me by,
You say you don't even care.
But I could always recognize a real good-bye,
And I know your heart's not there.
We've had our differences, we're still the same,
Hear what we want to hear.
Now I'm head over heels in the lost and found.
It's a cryin' shame, I thought we made the perfect pair.
(To Chorus:)

PAPA LOVED MAMA

Words and Music by
KIM WILLIAMS and GARTH BROOKS

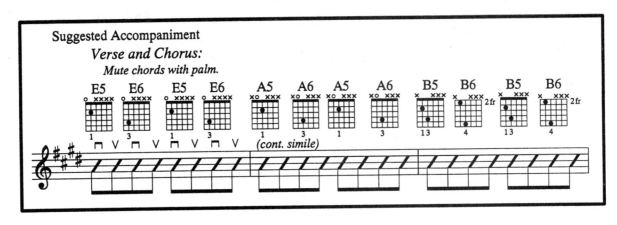

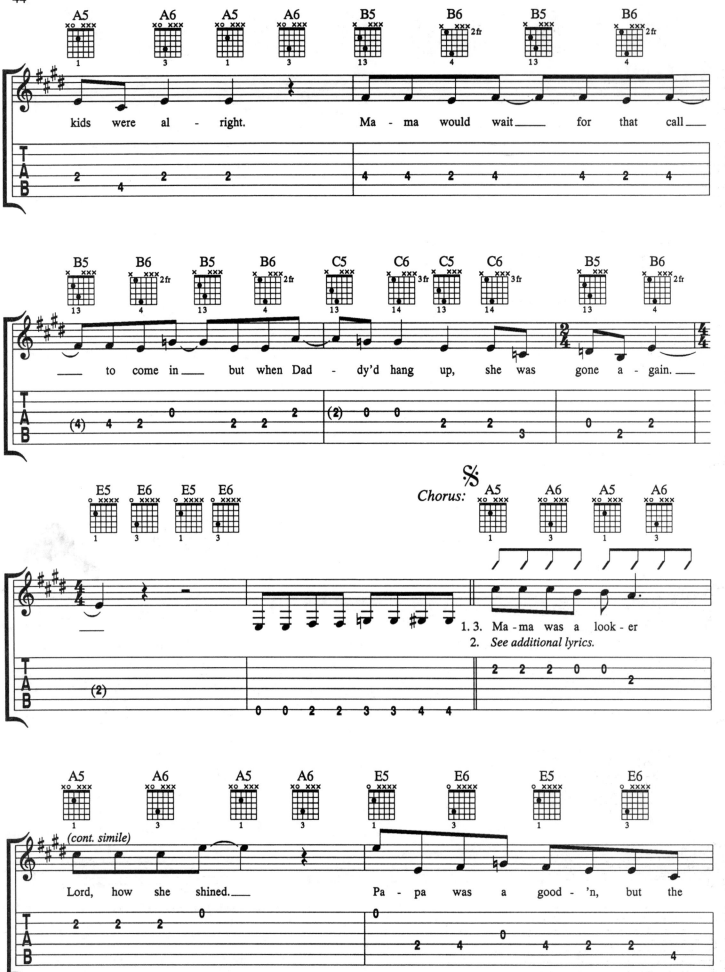

Verse 2:
Well, it was bound to happen and one night it did,
Papa came home and it was just us kids.
He had a dozen roses and a bottle of wine,
If he was lookin' to surprise us, he was doin' fine.
I heard him cry for Mama up and down the hall,
Then I heard a bottle break against the bedroom wall.
That old diesel engine made an eerie sound,
When papa fired it up and headed into town.

Chorus 2:
Well, the picture in the paper showed the scene real well,
Papa's rig was buried in the local motel.
The desk clerk said he saw it all real clear.
He never hit the brakes and he was shifting gears.
(To Chorus 1:)

TEQUILA SUNRISE

Words and Music by
DON HENLEY and GLENN FREY

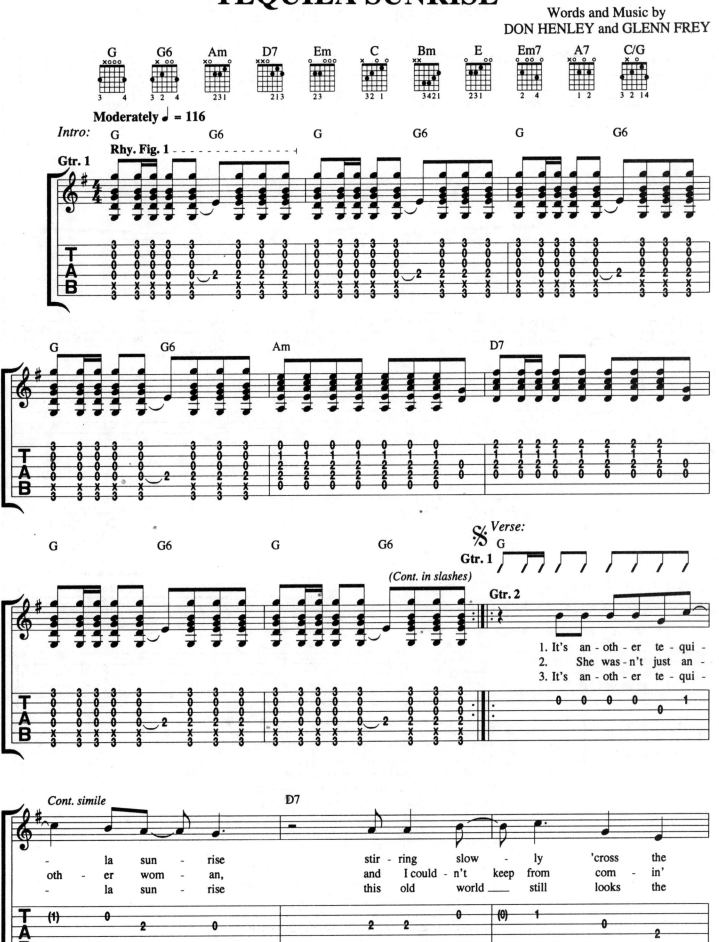

48

Tequila Sunrise – 3 – 2

RED STROKES

By
JAMES GARVER, LISA SANDERSON,
JENNY YATES and GARTH BROOKS

Verse 2:
Steam on the windows, salt in a kiss.
Two hearts have never pounded like this.
Inspired by a vision
That they can't command.
Erasing the boarders
With each brush of a hand.
(To Chorus 2:)

GUITAR TAB GLOSSARY **

TABLATURE EXPLANATION

READING TABLATURE: Tablature illustrates the six strings of the guitar. Notes and chords are indicated by the placement of fret numbers on a given string(s).

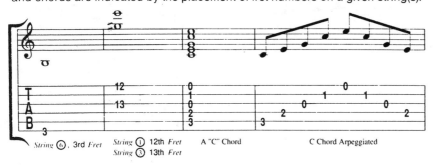

String ⑥, *3rd Fret* *String* ① *12th Fret* A "C" Chord C Chord Arpeggiated
String ③ *13th Fret*

BENDING NOTES

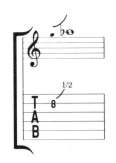

HALF STEP: Play the note and bend string one half step.*

WHOLE STEP: Play the note and bend string one whole step.

PREBEND AND RELEASE: Bend the string, play it, then release to the original note.

RHYTHM SLASHES

STRUM INDICA-TIONS: Strum with indicated rhythm. The chord voicings are found on the first page of the transcription underneath the song title.

INDICATING SINGLE NOTES USING RHYTHM SLASHES: Very often single notes are incorporated into a rhythm part. The note name is indicated above the rhythm slash with a fret number and a string indication.

*A half step is the smallest interval in Western music; it is equal to one fret. A whole step equals two frets.

**By Kenn Chipkin and Aaron Stang

ARTICULATIONS

HAMMER ON: Play lower note, then "hammer on" to higher note with another finger. Only the first note is attacked.

PULL OFF: Play higher note, then "pull off" to lower note with another finger. Only the first note is attacked.

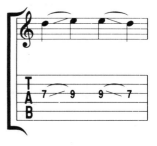

LEGATO SLIDE: Play note and slide to the following note. (Only first note is attacked).

PALM MUTE: The note or notes are muted by the palm of the pick hand by lightly touching the string(s) near the bridge.

ACCENT: Notes or chords are to be played with added emphasis.

DOWN STROKES AND UPSTROKES: Notes or chords are to be played with either a downstroke (⊓ ·) or upstroke (∨) of the pick.